Printed in Canada.

EFFECTIVE PRAYER LIFE

by Chuck Smith

THE WORD FOR TODAY

P.O. Box 8000, Costa Mesa, CA
92628

Effective Prayer Life
by Chuck Smith
Published by **The Word For Today**
P.O. Box 8000, Costa Mesa, CA 92628
(800) 272-WORD (9673)
http://www.thewordfortoday.org

© 1979, 1980, 1996, 2000 The Word For Today
ISBN 0–936728–03–2
(Previously registered ISBN 0–89337–008–8)

Unless otherwise indicated, Scripture quotations in this book are taken from the King James Version of the Bible. Translational emendations, amplifications, and paraphrases are by the author.

TABLE OF CONTENTS

INTRODUCTION

Today, we are living in desperate times. Yet, the Church is not desperate before God in prayer.

Jesus said to Peter, James, and John, *"What? Could you not watch with me one hour?"* (Matthew 26:40 NKJV). We say, "Shame on you, Peter! Shame on you, John! How terrible! Not watching with the Lord in prayer for even one hour!" But look out. Whenever you point a finger at someone else, there are three pointing back at you.

Prayer is the most important activity a born-again Christian can perform. It should head your list of priorities, for certainly the world around us desperately needs prayer. Prayer will open the door for God to do a glorious work in these last days. Prayer will stem the tide of evil.

This collection of studies on prayer presents you with certain Scriptures, thoughts, and rules. When you put them into practice in your life, they will bring you into a new relationship with God, and help you to experience a more effective and dynamic prayer life in which to do battle against the evil forces in these last days. We wrestle not against flesh and blood, but against spirit powers and principalities, thus the weapons of our warfare cannot be carnal. Prayer is the most potent weapon that we possess in our spiritual arsenal and by it we can pull down the strongholds of the enemy. Does Satan have a stronghold on your city government? Does he have a stronghold on your husband or wife or children? Through this book you will learn how to break down these strongholds.

CHAPTER 1

WHAT IS PRAYER?

Prayer can be expressed in three basic forms: worship, petition, and intercession; with variations within each form.

Worship

The first basic form of prayer is worship. It is a spontaneous result from the conscious awareness of God. As I realize the greatness of God and His nearness to me and His love for

3

me, I naturally respond with deep, inner worship of Him. One day I watched a little gnat flying around. I was amazed at how small it was, and yet so wonderfully designed. He was able to defy the laws of gravity, suspending himself in the air and then darting around rapidly. I thought, "God you are so wise in the design of even small forms of life."

Worshipping God for His creative genius is a form of prayer—that consciousness of who He is and what He has done inspires worship. When I recognize the wisdom and power of God, I stand in awe of Him. Thanksgiving and praise arise spontaneously as I become conscious of the goodness of God to me that I know I do not deserve.

Christians should engage in this form of communion and prayer constantly. We should become more conscious of Him as He speaks to us through nature. We see His power in the storm and lightning. We smell His loveliness in a rose. We see His design in a daisy. "In the rustling grass, I hear Him pass, He speaks to me everywhere." Sometimes we verbalize our worship; often we don't. It's simply an overwhelming feeling within our hearts as God manifests Himself to us in a thousand different ways. We just say, "Ohhh, God is so good!" We worship Him and commune with Him in the recognition of His love and grace.

Petition

The second form of prayer is petition, as I bring my personal needs before God and ask Him for the help that I need so desperately. Day by day I cry out to the Lord for His wisdom, guidance, strength, and provision. There are some people who dismiss personal petition prayer as selfish. They say that it's wrong to pray for anything for yourself because you ought to be thinking more of others.

As part of my initiation into the Hi Y Club in Jr. High I had to memorize this poem.

> *Lord, let me live from day to day,*
> *In such a self-forgetting way,*
> *That even when I kneel to pray,*
> *My prayer will be for others. Help me in all the*
> *things I do,*
> *To ever be sincerely true,*
> *To know that all I do for You,*
> *Must needs be done for others.*
> *Others, Lord, yes others,*

Let this my motto be.
Help me to live for others,
That I might live for Thee.

It is beautiful poetry that expresses truth. I should pray for others and be concerned with their needs. Nevertheless, I must also be concerned in prayer with my own needs. Call it what you want, but I have certain definite needs that must be met before I can be of benefit to others.

The Bible says, *"The husbandman that laboureth must be first partaker of the fruits"* (2 Timothy 2:6). In other words, you can't give what you don't have. Like measles, you can't give 'em unless you got 'em. Therefore, I must first be a partaker of God's grace, love, strength, and power. Then, as I partake, I have something to share with others.

One of Jesus' disciples said, *"Lord, teach us to pray, as John also taught his disciples."* Jesus then taught that model prayer: *"Our Father which art in heaven, Hallowed be thy name. Thy kingdom come. Thy will be done, as in heaven so in earth"* (Luke 11:1-2). The first part of the prayer is addressed to God— worshipping God for what He is: *"Hallowed be thy name."* Then comes the prayer for the kingdom of God: *"Thy kingdom come."* We are to seek first the kingdom of God and His righteousness.

The very next petition is *"Give us day by day our daily bread…and lead us not into temptation, but deliver us from evil"* (Luke 11:3–4). These are personal petitions for my own needs. I do have needs, and God wants me to bring those needs before Him. There's nothing wrong with praying and asking God to supply my rent money or whatever else I might need.

Intercession

The third form of prayer, intercession, is the type of prayer that can be considered work. Worshipping God is not work—that's glorious! It's spontaneous, beautiful communion and fellowship with God. Petition isn't too much work because I'm so interested in what I need that I can become involved in it very easily. But when I begin to intercede, then I must labor.

Paul, in his closing remarks to the church at Colosse, makes mention of one of his fellow laborers, Epaphras. *"Epaphras, who is one of you, a servant of Christ, saluteth you, always laboring fervently for you in prayers"* (Colossians 4:12). Here prayer is described as work.

Through intercessory prayer I reach out beyond myself and pray, not for my own needs, but for the needs of those around me. I pray for my family, friends, and neighbors who don't yet know Jesus Christ. I pray for the needs of those in the Body of Christ. I bring before God all the various needs of others that have come to my attention.

It is during intercessory prayer that I become aware of what prayer actually is: a spiritual battle.

The Battle

There's a conflict taking place around us continually, a spiritual conflict. Invisible to our physical eyes is the spirit world which is divided into two categories: the forces of good and the forces of evil. These are in constant combat with one another and diametrically opposed to each other. When I enter into intercessory prayer I step right into the battle and begin to fight in this spiritual warfare.

Paul the apostle said that *"we wrestle not against flesh and blood, but against principalities, against powers, against the rulers of the darkness of this world, against spiritual wickedness in high places"* (Ephesians 6:12). Therefore, we're to put on the whole armor of God. Paul then goes on to list the armor of God that should clothe a Christian for battle.

For, the apostle said, the weapons of our warfare are not carnal, because we're not in a physical battle. If we were, then we'd have worldly weapons. But because we're in a spiritual battle, the weapons and armor of our warfare must be spiritual. Through them we pull down the strongholds of the enemy (2 Corinthians 10:4).

Once you're fully equipped with all this spiritual armor of Ephesians 6, what are you to do? Just stand there? No! Get into the fight! How do you get into the fight? *"Praying always with all prayer and supplication in the Spirit"* (Ephesians 6:18). You've been girded for the battle—now go to it!

Battle Scenario

The scene of the spiritual conflict is right here on the earth. The purpose of the conflict is the control of the earth and the individual lives upon it.

The earth rightfully belongs to Jesus Christ. He created it and gave it to man. But man forfeited it to Satan. Jesus came and purchased it back for Himself. He redeemed us and the world through His blood at Calvary. For a while as Jesus hung on the cross, Satan thought he was the victor. But on the third day Jesus rose again, triumphing over death, hell, the grave, and Satan.

John tells us in 1 John 3:8 that Jesus was manifested to destroy the works of the devil. This He did through His death on the cross (Hebrews 2:14). He conquered Satan's forces—spoiled the principalities and powers that were against us, nailed them to His cross, triumphed over them, and made an open display of His victory (Colossians 2:14,15). Though the world rightfully belongs to Jesus Christ now, Satan seeks to maintain control and power over it by force. Much as when God had rejected King Saul from reigning over Israel and had the prophet Samuel anoint David in his stead, Saul, by force, tried to hold on to that which was no longer rightfully his, and sought to drive David from the kingdom. So Satan seeks to hold on to that which is no longer rightfully his.

Jesus Christ also has a method of winning the world, but not by force. Jesus seeks to draw men unto Himself and into His kingdom through love. Thus, the warfare continues in this world for the control of individual lives. Satan applies tremendous force and pressure to keep people in his camp. Jesus, wooing and drawing through gentle love, seeks to persuade men to submit their lives to Him.

As you enter into intercessory prayer, you rush into the thick of the battle. It becomes work because you're engaged against the forces of darkness and hell. You're going against the enemy's strongholds with prayer. You witness the grip of power that Satan has on the lives of those around you. Through prayer you can advance with the battering ram and demolish the strongholds the enemy has on those individual lives—freeing them from the power by which he holds them captive.

This kind of prayer, the warfare praying in the Spirit, becomes real work. You begin to understand what Paul meant when he said that

Epaphras was "laboring fervently" in prayer. It's wonderful to realize that prayer is the deciding factor in this spiritual warfare.

Satan is a very stubborn enemy and an obstinate fighter. He yields only what and when he must. Therefore, your prayers must be very specific. Vague, general prayers like "God, save the world" won't even dent the enemy. But when you bring an individual before the Lord, laying claim to that person for Jesus Christ, you begin to be specific in prayer, and Satan must yield.

"Lord, my friend, John, is bound by the power of Satan. His life is being ruined and twisted. I come against that work of Satan in the name of Jesus Christ and in the victory of the cross of Jesus Christ. I ask you, Father, to free him from this power of Satan that's holding him today. Loose him now, that he may know the love of Jesus Christ. Lord, let your Spirit speak to his heart and bring an end to the work of Satan that's binding him, and blinding him." We thus recover them from the snare of the devil that is holding them as captives.

Realize that Satan is persistent. Even after you begin to see a bit of victory, you must continue in prayer to hold the ground that you've gained. The minute you win ground, Satan will turn right around and counterattack to regain it. Your prayers must be persistent. The ground we have taken from the enemy through prayer, must be held by prayer. Many times we make a serious mistake when we begin seeing signs of victory in the life of one for whom we have been interceding. Maybe they have gone forward to receive Christ and have started to read their Bibles, so we quit praying for them. Often the seed has not had a chance to take root yet and the enemy comes to take away the seed. We need to continue to pray long after we begin to see initial signs of victory.

The beautiful truth is that Satan has already been defeated. As we go into battle the outcome has already been determined. Jesus triumphed over Satan and, thus, Satan must yield when we come against him in the power and in the authority of Jesus Christ. Lay claim to the victory in Jesus Christ—and life after life will be set free as you come against the strongholds of Satan and tear them down with this powerful weapon of prayer!

God has made prayer available to the weakest of His children. It's something that every Christian can exercise, regardless of his spiritual state. You don't have to be a spiritual giant to get into spiritual warfare. And you don't have to be afraid of the enemy as you enter in, because he's already been defeated.

Satan knows that prayer spells his defeat. He'll fight you more to keep you from prayer than any other thing you do. Sometimes, he even encourages you to other specific activities because he knows how fruitless they are.

You'll be amazed at the disturbances that come your way when you kneel down and start praying. The telephone will ring. Or someone will be at the front door. Or you'll suddenly remember something you've been wanting to do. When I pray I usually take a notepad with me so I can jot down those thoughts of the forgotten things that need attention. Otherwise I'm tempted to get up and do them immediately. Satan will do anything to get you away from prayer.

Intercessory prayer is a real labor. It's a real conflict in the battle against Satan. It's the deciding factor, and that's why Satan fights it so hard.

Suppose that someone attacked you on a dark street and started wrestling with you. If he were to pull a knife, the whole battle would suddenly be centered on one thing—control of the knife. All of a sudden, you'd forget about punching him in the nose. You'd be grabbing for his wrist and trying to knock that knife out of his hand for you realize that it is the deciding factor in this battle.

Satan knows that prayer brings you victory and spells his defeat. He knows it's the deciding factor in this spiritual warfare. That's why he concentrates all his efforts against prayer. He'll do all he can to upset your prayer time, and keep you from praying.

Persistence

If the answers to your prayers don't come immediately, don't give up! Paul speaks of Epaphras "laboring fervently" in prayer for the Colossians (Colossians 4:12). I don't believe that Epaphras said, "O Lord, bless the Church in Colosse, in Jesus' name. Amen." Rather, he waited upon God, diligently sought after God for the welfare and the benefit of that church, and continued the practice of prayer day after day. James 5:16 speaks of effective fervent prayer availing much.

Many times we give up a little bit too soon. Whenever Satan begins losing his grip he makes a last, desperate lunge. This is when we all too often become tired and give up, quitting just short of victory.

In his book, *How to Win Friends and Influence People*, Mr. Carnigie tells of a Mr. Darby, a wealthy insurance broker from the East, who was caught up with gold fever and headed out to Colorado. He did some prospecting and discovered a very rich vein of gold in the Rockies. He returned to the East and convinced all his friends to invest their money in a mining venture. They formed a corporation, bought a great deal of equipment, and mined this very wealthy vein of gold ore in Colorado.

About the time that the corporation paid off all its debts, the vein of gold ran out. The investors kept digging until they ran themselves into debt again. Finally one day, a discouraged Mr. Darby ordered an end to the digging. He closed the mine, went into Denver, and sold the mine and equipment to a junk dealer for a few hundred dollars. Mr. Darby headed back home.

The junk dealer hired a geologist to study the mine and the area. The geologist came back with a report: "If you'll dig three feet past the point where Mr. Darby quit, you'll find that same vein of gold." The junk dealer became the wealthiest mine owner in the state of Colorado. Just three more feet! I wonder how many times we, too, stop three feet short of victory.

Claim the Promises

There are many fantastic promises given to us about prayer through Jesus Christ.

> *Verily I say unto you, Whatsoever ye shall bind on earth shall be bound in heaven; and whatsoever ye shall loose on earth shall be loosed in heaven....if two of you shall agree on earth as touching any thing that they shall ask, it shall be done for them of my Father which is in heaven.*
>
> —Matthew 18:18–19

The number in prayer: any two of you. The place of prayer: on earth. The scope of prayer: any thing. *"It shall be done for them of my Father which is in heaven."* That is a broad and glorious promise!

Jesus also promised:

*Have faith in God. For verily I say unto you,
That whosoever shall say unto this mountain, Be
thou removed, and be thou cast into the sea; and
shall not doubt in his heart, but shall believe that
those things which he saith shall come to pass; he
shall have whatsoever he saith. Therefore I say
unto you, What things soever ye desire, when ye
pray, believe that ye receive them, and ye shall
have them.*

—Mark 11:22–24

What a fantastic promise! Also, Jesus said,

*And whatsoever ye shall ask in my name, that
will I do, that the Father may be glorified in the
Son. If ye shall ask any thing in my name, I will
do it.*

—John 14:13–14

Any thing!

Another promise: "*If ye abide in me, and my
words abide in you, ye shall ask what ye will, and it
shall be done unto you*" (John 15:7). Also,
"*Whatsoever ye shall ask the Father in my name, he
will give it [to] you. Hitherto have ye asked nothing
in my name: ask* [the Greek is intensive— 'please
ask'], *and ye shall receive, that your joy may be full*"

(John 16:23–24). Here the Lord is begging you to ask Him anything and He said He will do it.

These are extremely broad promises to prayer. But to whom were the promises made? Jesus wasn't talking here to the multitudes. In every case Jesus was talking to His disciples.

Who qualifies as a disciple? Jesus said, *"If any man will come after me, let him deny himself, and take up his cross, and follow me"* (Matthew 16:24). A person who has denied himself, taken up the cross, and is following Jesus Christ can take these promises and lay claim to them. Anything he asks, desires, or wishes will be done.

But, by the very virtue of the fact that a disciple has denied himself, he is not seeking the things that would glorify his flesh. The very fact that he's taken up his cross, he's not seeking his own glory, but reckoning himself to be dead with Christ. He is now identified only in the things that God wants: committing himself, his ambitions, and his life totally to Jesus Christ. The true thrust of prayer is always, *"Nevertheless, not what I will, but Thy will be done."*

Only by denying yourself, taking up your cross, and following Jesus Christ do you receive access to the powerful promises of God regarding your prayers.

When the Answer Is No

The Lord may not give us what we ask when He has a higher purpose in mind for our lives.

Moses prayed that God would allow him to go into the Promised Land. God said, "No, Moses. For the sake of the people you can't go into the land. You misrepresented Me before those people. Now they must learn the lesson of obedience." Moses, that mighty spiritual giant who communed face to face with God, wasn't allowed to go into the Promised Land (Numbers 20:7–12).

Throughout the centuries since then, parents have told their children the story of Moses, the man of God, who was used by God to deliver the children of Israel from Egypt and bring them to their own land. They tell of Moses who went up into the mountain and received the law of God in the midst of the fire and rolling thunder; whose face shone so that he had to cover himself with a veil; who stretched forth the rod and the Red Sea parted. Then with whispered tones they would say to their children, "But Moses could not go into the land because he disobeyed God." In order to teach the future generations of the nation of Israel the lesson of the importance of complete obedience, God did not answer Moses' prayer.

I think of Paul's thorn in the flesh. He said, *"I besought the Lord thrice that it might depart from me."* But God didn't deliver him. Why? God had given Paul an abundance of revelations, and that thorn in the flesh was necessary to keep him humbled. *"There was given to me a thorn in the flesh, the messenger of Satan to buffet me, lest I should be exalted above measure."* Paul said, *"Most gladly therefore will I rather glory in my infirmities, that the power of Christ may rest upon me"* (2 Corinthians 12:7–10). Actually, Paul learned to rejoice over that rotten thorn, because he experienced the mighty power of God as a result of the infirmity.

Consider the prayer of Jesus that wasn't answered. Though He prayed three times— *"Father, if it be possible, let this cup pass from me"* (Matthew 26:39)—He drank the cup. Why?

Because God wanted to bring salvation to each one of us. It should be noted that Jesus, though offering His prayer to the Father, added what is so important to every prayer: *"Nevertheless not my will, but thine, be done"* (Luke 22:42). That is the key to obedience and prayer. "Lord, here's what I want. Here's my desire. Nevertheless, not my will, but Thy will be done." You can't improve on that! For the real purpose of prayer is never to get my will done, but His.

Ineffective Prayers

Many prayers are ineffective, they seemingly, produce nothing. They go up and yet they bring nothing down. God does answer prayer. That's the inspiration behind all prayer; for if God never answered prayer, no one would be praying anymore. But why have so many prayers been offered without achieving any results?

Certain things can actually hinder your prayers from being effective. First of all, if you harbor sin within your life your prayers are hindered. Isaiah declared,

> *The LORD's hand is not shortened, that it cannot save; neither his ear heavy, that it cannot hear:*

*but your iniquities have separated between you
and your God.*

—Isaiah 59:1–2

So many times when my prayers aren't
answered I want to blame God. In reality, the
fault is mine. There's sin at my door. David said
that if I regard iniquity in my heart, the Lord
does not hear me when I pray (Psalm 66:18).

Sin, as Isaiah said, breaks your connection
with God. It's like cutting the telephone cord.
You may dial the number all you want. You
may speak in eloquent and very persuasive
terms. Yet, you've cut the cord. The message is
simply going into the ground and not getting
anywhere.

At that point prayer becomes deceptive.
Many people say, "I know I'm not living as I
should be, but I still pray." But their prayers are
of no value. Their relationship with God has
been severed because of the sin within their
lives. Their sins have separated them from their
God.

Another cause for ineffective prayers is an
unforgiving spirit. Jesus taught so much about
forgiveness. When He gave us the model prayer
He emphasized one point at the end. If you

won't forgive men their trespasses, neither will your Father in heaven forgive you your trespasses (Matthew 6:15). It's important to forgive, for you cannot come to God harboring a grudge against a brother without hindering your own prayers to God.

Ineffective prayers can also be a result of selfish motivation. James said, *"Ye have not, because ye ask not"* (James 4:2). It's true that in many cases you just haven't prayed. Many times a person will pour out their horrible tale of woe to me. I'll ask, "Have you prayed?" "Well, no." But that's where you start! You have not because you ask not.

Then James went on to say, *"Ye ask, and receive not..."*—here comes the rub—*"because ye ask amiss, that ye may consume it upon your lusts"* (James 4:3). Behind so many prayers are selfish desires.

When I was in high school I prayed that God would give me a beautiful little '36 customized Ford. Oh, how I lusted after that car! I told God all the good things I'd do for Him— all the kids I would pick up for Sunday school—if He'd just give me that car. How could He miss?

I didn't get it, and I know why. God could see that in the back of my mind I was cruising around the high school rapping those Smitty mufflers and getting the attention of all those good-looking girls on campus. God knew that a customized '36 Ford would have puffed me up with pride. So He gave me a Model A.

So many of our prayers are self-centered. As I mentioned earlier, there are needs that I have and God wants to supply them. I should pray for them, but I must be careful lest all my prayers have only self as the underlying motive.

Helpful Hints

Here are a few rules for prayer that I have found to be effective. First of all, make the will of God your prayer. How? Discover the will of God through the Word of God. God has declared to you His will, purpose, and plan in the Bible. Give place to the Scriptures in your prayers. Too many times prayer is only a monologue—and you're doing all the talking. But that isn't communion. Communion is a dialogue, talking and listening while God speaks to you in His Word.

Tell God your needs and the needs of others around you. Express to Him what you see, what you feel, and what you desire. Then turn to the Word, and God will speak to you. He'll minister to you and show you His will and plan for your life.

Then come again to Him: "Well, Lord, here it is in Your Word. I can see this is what You desire so I claim it in the name of Jesus Christ." Listen and learn to hear the voice of God as He speaks to you by His Spirit. In Genesis 32 when Jacob heard that his brother Esau, who had vowed to kill him, was coming to meet him with four hundred men, he feared for his life. He was driven to pray and as he prayed he reminded God of His promise. He said, *"O God of my father Abraham...the Lord which saidst unto me, Return unto thy country and to thy kindred, and I will deal well with thee"* (Genesis 32:9). Jacob was praying on the basis of God's word to him.

Prayer is to be addressed to the Father, in the authority of the name of Jesus. Actually, you have no right to an audience with God on your own. There's no way you can earn such a privilege. The only way you can have an audience with the Father is through Jesus Christ.

Jesus said, *"I am the way, the truth, and the life: no man cometh unto the Father, but by me"* (John 14:6).

Ask the Father for your needs, but ask Him in the name of Jesus Christ. It's through Jesus Christ that you have the right to come, that you have a hearing, and are received. When you knock, use the name of Jesus. If I knock on His door and say, "Father, it's Chuck here, wanting to talk to you."

He is apt to respond, "Who's Chuck, what right do you have to knock on My door?"

But if when I knock I say, "Father, this is Chuck and I come in the name of Jesus." The response will be, "Come on in Chuck, good to hear from you."

Use Your Weapons

More victories are wrought through prayer than any other means. It's shocking that, though God has given us such a powerful weapon, we are defeated again and again— The problem is, though we possess the weapon we seldom use it.

As Christians, we're so often trying to defend our weapons. For instance, when people argue against the Bible, we begin to defend it. The Bible is a great weapon, a sharp two-edged sword. Don't defend it, use it! If you're in a duel, you don't say: "You had better watch out, this sword has the sharpest steel in town. It's been honed to a super-fine edge." You don't defend your sword. You use your sword!

Likewise, we're always talking about our weapon of prayer. Don't talk about prayer. *Pray.* Use the weapons that God has given you and triumph over the enemy!

CHAPTER 2

THE PURPOSE OF PRAYER

How we need to pray! Not talk about it. Not have conferences about it. But to actually practice the privilege of prayer.

Paul said, *"Continue in prayer"* (Colossians 4:2). The Greek word for "continue" speaks of persistence and constancy. Continue steadfastly in prayer.

Why is persistence necessary in prayer? Some people say that praying for the same need more than once shows a lack of faith on our part. Yet, in the Garden of Gethsemane Jesus prayed the same prayer three times (Matthew 26:39–44).

Also, in speaking of his own thorn in the flesh, Paul the apostle said, *"For this thing I besought the Lord thrice, that it might depart from me"* (2 Corinthians 12:8).

Jesus taught persistence in prayer in two parables. In the first one He said, *"Men ought always to pray, and not to faint"* (Luke 18:1). He then illustrated this by the story of a callous judge and a determined widow. The widow visited the judge every day saying, *"Avenge me of mine adversary."*

The judge, even though he did not fear God or man, said, "This woman will drive me crazy by coming here every day!" So, he wrote out his judgment in her favor. Then Jesus added, *"Shall not God avenge his own elect...? I tell you that he will avenge them speedily"* (Luke 18:2–8).

At first I found difficulty with the fact that Jesus used an unjust judge as a comparison with our just God. But the parable actually shows a vast contrast. If an unjust judge could be persuaded to act by the persistence of a woman, how much more will our fair and loving Father bring about a just and speedy judgment for those who are calling upon Him.

The other parable about persistence in prayer concerns a fellow who heard a knock on his door at midnight. He opened the door to find some of his friends had come to spend the night. Wanting to feed them before he bedded them down, he went to the cupboard but found he didn't have enough bread. So, he went to his neighbor's house, knocked on the door, and said, "Open up and give me some bread! I've got company."

The neighbor replied, "I'm already in bed with my wife and children. Come back tomorrow." But the fellow kept knocking and wouldn't stop until he had what he needed. Because of this man's importunity, the neighbor finally got up and gave him the bread (Luke 11:5–10).

We see that the Bible teaches persistence in prayer. Does that mean our prayers persuade God to do things our way? Does God have an arbitrary reluctance to answer us, and we make

Him give in to our demands by being persistent and obnoxious? I hardly think so.

I am convinced that prayers do not and cannot change the purposes of God—though you pray fervently, though you petition with tears, though you pray for days. God is far too loving to give in just because you are weeping and persevering for something He knows would be detrimental to you and would destroy you in the end.

Prayer doesn't change the purpose of God, but prayer can change the action of God.

Jesus said, *"Your Father knows the things you have need of, before you ask him"* (Matthew 6:8 NKJV). Your prayers aren't for the purpose of informing God of your situation. He knows all your needs before you ever ask Him. But your prayers open the door and allow God the opportunity to do those things that He's been desiring to do, but wouldn't do in violation of your own free will.

In John 15:16, Jesus said to His disciples,

You did not choose Me, but I chose you and appointed you that you should go and bear fruit, and that your fruit should remain, that whatever

you ask the Father in My name, He may give you
(NKJV).

Note, He *may* give it to you. God knows
your needs and desires to meet them. Prayer
opens the door to allow Him to do those things
He desires to do. It is giving God my consent to
do what He desires in my life. God has given me
a free will and will not violate my free will.
Thus, I must ask in order to receive.

God knows that in one year I will need a
particular thing, because He knows all my exact
needs in advance. I don't know my needs even a
month from now. If God gave me today what I'll
need in a year, then I might not use it as He
intends it to be used.

So, as I become aware of my needs, I cry out
to God, "Help me and meet this need now." I
have finally become aware of the problem. But
God has been aware of it all the time. Now
when I ask Him for help, He is free to give it to
me because I'll use it as He wants it to be used.

God's Timing

Sometimes our prayers are answered almost
as quickly as they're spoken. Eliezer the servant
was sent by Abraham on a special mission: to

find a wife for Isaac. As he came to a certain well, Eliezer said, "Lord, let a young virgin come here to draw water and when I say to her, 'Give me a drink.' Let her answer, 'Not only will I give you a drink, but I'll also draw water for your camels.' And Lord, let her be the one you have chosen as a bride for Isaac."

While the servant was yet praying in his heart, a young girl came to the well to draw water. He said to her, "Give me a drink." She quickly let the water jug down from her head, gave him a drink, and then said, "Not only thee but I will also draw for thy camels." And she drew water for the camels (Genesis 24:1–20).

This is one of those beautiful, instantaneous answers to prayer that always thrills us. No sooner do the prayers escape the heart than God is answering them.

It is also true that we have prayed many years for certain needs and have not seen the answer.

Why is it that some prayers are answered immediately and others seem to be delayed? We pray for some people and they're healed. We pray for others and they die.

First of all, this demonstrates that we're not in control of the situation. God is in control and He does according to His own purpose and will. Prayers should never be thought of as changing the purposes of God.

We have a very wrong concept of prayer when we think of it as changing God's mind, altering God's purposes, or getting my will done. The true purpose of prayer is to get God's will done—to open the door for God to accomplish that which He has purposed to do.

Thus, we are led to the conclusion that true prayer begins in the heart of God. God makes known to me what is His purpose, His desire, His wishes. I offer it back to God in prayer, and the cycle is completed. When I pray in this manner, I am in harmony with God's will. In 1 John 5:14,15 we read,

> *And this is the confidence that we have in Him, that, if we ask any thing according to His will He heareth us: and if we know that He hear us whatsoever we ask, we know that we have the petitions that we desired of Him.*

Actually, *I* am the one often changed by prayer. Many times as I am praying God will speak to me. He will show me His way and His plan, which is always so much better than what I had in mind. While in prayer, God deals with me and shows me the folly of certain things that I have been insisting, and practically demanding, from Him. I respond, "Thank you, Lord, for not answering me during the last five years." He knew what was best for me all the time! At this point in my life, as I look back, I am as thankful for the prayers He did not answer as those He did.

God has a plan for this earth, and He has chosen human instruments to do His work. Some people say that God can only work through man. That's not true. God has chosen to use man. God could work in any way He wants. He is not limited by human instruments. If we fail, God isn't going to fail. At times in history God has used angels to do His work on earth, such as the destruction of Sodom and Gomorrah.

We must not lay the heavy responsibility of thwarting God's purpose on any person. We sometimes hear said, "If you fail to help in the purposes of God, the program of God is going to fail, and you'll be responsible! You'll have to stand before God and answer for that failure!"

That isn't true. God will accomplish His purpose one way or another.

By choosing to use you to do His will, God is giving you the blessed opportunity of knowing the joy of working together with Him. Then, as results begin to take place, He rewards you as though you did the work! When you get to heaven you'll be rewarded for those accomplishments, even though it was God who did the whole thing!

When the survival of the Jewish race was being threatened by a cruel edict, Mordecai told Esther, "If you at this point hold your peace, deliverance will come from another quarter. But you'll be destroyed" (Esther 4:14). He was warning her that when they try to wipe out the Jews, she would not escape the edict, even though she was in the palace.

Likewise, when you fail to do God's will, deliverance will come from another quarter. You'll lose the blessing and the reward of being a co-laborer with God, but God's program and purpose will not fail.

God Wants to Bless You

Second Chronicles tells us of King Asa's calling upon the Lord. When he first came to the throne, the King was faced with a very difficult situation—the Ethiopians had invaded the land with a million-man army and 300 chariots. King Asa cried out to God,

> LORD, *it is nothing with thee to help, whether with many, or with them that have no power: help us, O* LORD *our God; for we rest on thee, and in thy name we go against this multitude. O* LORD, *thou art our God; let not man prevail against thee.*
>
> —2 Chronicles 14:11

He knew the odds against him surviving meant nothing to God. If God be for us, who can be against us? God and you make a majority. The Lord was with Asa, and the king went out and destroyed the Ethiopian armies.

When King Asa returned from victory the prophet Azariah met him and said,

> *The* LORD *is with you, while ye be with him; and if ye seek him, he will be found of you; but if ye forsake him, he will forsake you.*
>
> —2 Chronicles 15:2

Asa began to prosper. He became very strong and powerful. In the later years of his reign he was threatened again. But this time, the threat came from Baasha, the king of the northern tribes of Israel, who was building fortified cities north of Jerusalem in preparation for an invasion. King Asa took money out of the treasury and sent it to hire Ben-Hadad, the king of Syria, to invade Israel from the north. This caused Baasha to withdraw his troops from invading Judah and to deploy them to defend the northern border. It was a clever and successful strategy that worked. However, rather than seeking the Lord in prayer, he sought human help. The prophet Hanani came to him and rebuked him for seeking the aid of man rather than the help of God. The prophet reminded him of how the Lord had helped him against the Ethiopians at the beginning of his reign, and he declared,

> *For the eyes of the LORD run to and fro throughout the whole earth, to show himself strong in the behalf of them whose heart is perfect toward him*

> —2 Chronicles 16:9

Here the Bible is declaring one of the basic truths of God. He is looking for people to bless.

God wants to work in your life and bless you. He wants to use you as one of His channels, as one of His instruments. But He's waiting for you to come into alignment with His plan. The moment your life comes into harmony with the purposes of God, you become a channel through which God's power and love can flow to a needy world.

God is looking for people whose hearts are in tune with His desires. Thus, the greatest prayer is "Lord, bring me into harmony with Thy will." You can't improve on that. But it has to be more than just lip service. It must come from the heart. And that's not easy.

There are so many things I want done, and so many of my prayers reflect selfishness. So many of my petitions are for things that would bring me comfort, ease, and happiness. *But the real purpose of prayer is to see the work of God accomplished in my life and then, through my life, in the lives of others.*

I believe that God intends to give you every right thing that you pray for, but His timing is often different than yours. Many times God delays the answers to your prayers for a very good reason.

One reason God may delay an answer to your prayer is that He desires to give you more than what you were asking for at the moment.

Hannah is a good example of this. She had been barren for years. Her husband had another wife with many children. Day after day Hannah's barrenness plagued her.

One day Hannah and her husband were traveling to the tabernacle while the other wife stayed at home with the kids. On their journey to Shiloh her husband asked, "Hannah, why are you so sad?"

Hannah replied, "Give me children."

He responded, "Am I God that I could give you children? Aren't I better to you than many sons? Aren't you satisfied with me?"

When Hannah arrived at the tabernacle the agony of her heart was so great that she couldn't even utter her request. She felt the grief so deeply that she just lay before God in the court of the tabernacle. Her lips were moving, but she made no sound with her voice.

Eli the priest passed by and saw Hannah prostrate before the Lord. He thought she was drunk and ordered her to stay away from wine. Hannah said, "No, I am not drunk. But the handmaiden of the Lord is grieved because she is barren. I've been pleading with God to give me a son. If He will give me a son, I have promised to give him back to God all the days of his life" (1 Samuel 1).

That's what God wanted to hear from Hannah, because God needed a man. The state of the nation Israel was so corrupt that there wasn't a man around for God to use. Before God could get a man, He had to get a woman. Therefore, He dealt with Hannah's heart.

Hannah had been praying for a son for many years—a son for her own joy and pleasure, a son that would put an end to the taunts from the other wife. Hannah had prayed, "Lord, give me a son. Take away the shame." But finally she prayed, "Lord, give me a son. And I'll give him back to You all the days of his life." Hannah had finally come into harmony with the purposes of God.

The priest told her, "Go in peace. The Lord has heard your prayer. You will have a son." Hannah went home and God gave her a son, Samuel. He became a prophet, a priest, and one of the most outstanding leaders of God's people in the Old Testament.

Yes, God wanted to give Hannah a son all the while. But He delayed the answer to her prayers, so that He might work in her heart until she would be aligned with His purpose.

Do not get discouraged when God delays the answers to your prayers. He may want to give you so much more than what you've been asking for.

God knows the right time to answer our prayers. Jesus told His disciples to wait in Jerusalem until they receive:

> *The promise of the Father, which, saith he, ye have heard of me. For John truly baptized with water; but ye shall be baptized with the Holy Ghost not many days hence...ye shall receive power, after that the Holy Ghost is come upon you: and ye shall be witnesses unto me both in Jerusalem, and in all Judea, and in Samaria, and unto the uttermost part of the earth.*
>
> —Acts 1:4–5,8

After Jesus spoke these things, while His followers were standing with Him on the Mount of Olives in Bethany, He ascended into heaven, and a cloud received Him out of their sight.

The disciples returned to Jerusalem and continued steadfastly in prayer in one accord. The Bible says that they continued to wait till the day of Pentecost had fully come. It would have been possible for God to have poured out the Holy Spirit on them in the first ten minutes, but for His own purposes He saw fit to wait approximately seven days (Acts 1–2).

How long are you to persist in prayer? Until you get an answer—either a yes or no.

Pointers on Prayer

In Colossians Paul exhorts us to "watch," which literally means to "stay awake." Sleepiness is one of the weaknesses of our flesh while we pray. When Jesus was in the Garden of Gethsemane praying, He found His disciples asleep. He said, *"What, could ye not watch with me one hour?"* (Matthew 26:40). God wants our minds to be sharp and alert when we talk to Him. I think it's insulting to talk to God when our minds are half–awake.

Paul also exhorts us to pray "with thanksgiving" (Colossians 4:2). Our prayers should always be coupled with thanksgiving. The Psalms serve as an ideal example of this.

David prayed for everything in the Psalms—for himself, for his friends, and for his enemies. He also filled the Psalms with praises and thanksgiving unto God. They are as well-balanced with thanksgiving as with requests. Quite often, but not often enough, people come to me and say, "I don't have any problems to lay on you. I just wanted to praise the Lord with you! The Lord has been so good to me. I want to tell you how He's been blessing my life."

That's so exciting! I hear so many problems as a pastor that it's a great joy when someone says, "No problem. I just want to tell you the Lord is so good!" That's glorious!

It's a shame to continually lay some heavy problem on God. We ought to be thanking Him more for what He has already done for us.

In the early days of the United States the Puritans observed days of fasting and affliction. There was at least one day of fast each month of the year. Then someone said, "Let's have a day of thanksgiving! We won't fast or afflict ourselves, but we'll have a feast to thank the Lord for all He has done." Thus, Thanksgiving began.

Certainly, personal petitions are necessary in our prayers. But if I only pray when I have some desperate need in my own life and only bring personal petitions to God, I'm denying myself a fantastic blessing. Oh, that I would go to God with more praises and thanksgiving!

Paul also exhorts us to pray for ministers (Colossians 4:3). May God help the ministers. Often, people place ministers on a pedestal and make us into something we're not. We're all too human. I wish I were more of a saint, but I'm not!

Ministers have problems just like everybody else. We go through the same trials, perhaps to an even greater degree than most other Christians. Many times we're under heavier attacks by Satan because of our position of spiritual authority and leadership.

Ministers need prayer. Someone asked Spurgeon about his success. He answered, "My people pray for me." The Apostle Paul said, "Pray for us."

What did Paul want them to pray for him? He wanted them to pray that God would open a door of utterance (Colossians 4:3). At this point

Paul was in prison. You'd think that he would desire liberty. "Pray that God will open the door of the prison and get me out of this place!" Instead Paul prayed that God would open the door of opportunity to freely speak the Word.

Pray that God will help me not to be a powerless minister, but to be filled with His Spirit. Help me not to speak a lot, but say nothing. Pray that God will help me not to be a fantastic minister, speaking only to please and excite the people. Pray that I'll not be an idle minister, not being thoroughly furnished in the Word. Pray that I'll not be a cold minister and become unresponsive to the people's needs.

Pray that I might be a faithful minister speaking forth the mysteries of Christ, really demonstrating His love, setting an example before the flock, walking humbly before God as He would have me to do. Pray for your ministers. We covet your prayers. In turn, we'll pray for you.

CHAPTER 3

THE PRIVILEGE OF PRAYER

Everyone engages in prayer at one time or another. Even that person who says "I don't believe in God," cries out when the crisis looms, "O God, help me!" We are all acquainted with prayer to some extent or another.

Prayer is one of the greatest privileges God has given to man. It amazes me that I can come into the presence of God, the Creator of this universe, and talk with Him. And what's more—He always listens to me!

I'm also amazed that God has given me the privilege of talking with Him at any time. I don't have to make an appointment or call in advance. I can come at any hour, for any need, and open my heart before Him. And God not only listens, He's also promised to help me! He's promised to guide me and to provide for my every need.

I imagine one of the great mysteries among the angels in heaven is that man has been given this glorious privilege of prayer, yet he takes such little advantage of it and treats it in such a peculiar way.

Many people treat prayer as a religious work that they must do. After they have prayed for a time, they expect a merit badge for their work. "After all, I prayed a whole hour." As if one should be rewarded for talking to God!

Many people determine to pray an hour a day because it seems like an honorable thing to do. They start the hour of prayer by lifting up every request imaginable. Then, when ten minutes has gone by and they've run out of things to say, they start over again. They go through the list a few more times. Finally, the hour is over and they feel good. "Praise the Lord! I've spent a whole hour praying." They go their way convinced that they've done their duty and fulfilled their obligation.

Prayer should never be done by the clock. It should never be looked upon as an obligation, a required work, or a duty.

Remember, the length of your prayer isn't important at all. Often, there just isn't enough time for lengthy prayers. For instance, suppose that your car is stalled on the railroad tracks and the train is heading your way. If it takes a long prayer to do the job—you've had it!

Jesus warned us, *"When ye pray, use not vain repetitions, as the heathen do: for they think that they shall be heard for their much speaking"* (Matthew 6:7). Many people criticize the Catholics for their repetitious use of Hail Mary's and Our Fathers. But continually repeating, "Jesus! Jesus!" or "Glory! Glory!" or any other phrase is also using vain repetition. When you pray you're actually talking to the Father. You should talk to Him intelligently. Don't repeat the same words over and over again like a mantra. It will get you nowhere.

Scope of Prayer

The Christian has one source of power in his life: the Holy Spirit. Jesus said, *"Ye shall receive power, after that the Holy Ghost is come upon you"* (Acts 1:8). He is the source of power in your life.

However, your greatest outlet of spiritual power is prayer. I can do more for God through prayer than I can through any other means, including service. Prayer binds the strong man of the house, whereas service is going in and taking the spoil. I can do more than pray after I have prayed, but I really can't do more than pray until I have prayed. My service to God, though important, is limited to one place. Prayer, however, is limitless in its scope. It can reach around the world.

Through prayer I can spend one-half hour of my life in South America, doing work for the kingdom of God by strengthening the hands of the missionaries. Then I can go to Mexico and spend some time with my friends who are ministering there. I can help them in their ministry by praying for the effectiveness of the tracts they distribute and the words they speak. Then I can move into China and pray for the church there. I can touch a world for God through prayer right from my own closet.

Rewards

Jesus said, *"When you pray, don't be like the hypocrites"* (Matthew 6:5). The word hypocrite in Greek is *hupokrites*. The actors in classical Greek drama would wear character masks. These actors were called *hupokrites*.

In other words, Jesus said, "When you pray, don't be as one who merely puts on an act for the benefit of other people. Don't be as the *hupokrites* who like to pray standing in the synagogues and on street corners to be seen by men."

From this Scripture many people have assumed that public prayer is wrong. That's certainly not what Jesus said. Jesus himself prayed in public. The early Church also gathered together for public prayer. The Bible says the believers continued daily in the apostles' doctrine, fellowship, in the breaking of bread, and in prayers (Acts 2:42). Prayer is an essential part of our gathering together.

But be careful that you're not praying to impress men rather than to communicate to

God. This is an especially real danger for ministers, because we pray publicly so often. The real temptation comes at the close of a sermon, when I subtly repeat the major points of my message in the closing prayer to make sure the people understood it. I'm supposedly talking to God, but I'm actually trying to bring my point home to the people one more time.

In my early ministry I was almost ruined by public prayer. One day a lady said to me, "You pray the most beautiful prayers." So I thought, "I'll sharpen up on that. I'll make my prayers even more beautiful!" I became so interested in impressing people with the beauty of my prayers that I forgot I was actually talking to the Father.

There's a real danger in praying to impress people with how righteous, godly, and spiritually deep you think you are.

Jesus spoke of two rewards. The first one is given by men. It is given to the person who prays in public with the motivation of impressing people with how spiritual he is. He will be rewarded by someone saying, "Oh, he's so spiritual!"

The motivation of the Pharisees was just that—to make a display of their spirituality. On their way to the synagogue they acted as though they were consumed with spiritual zeal. They had to stop on the street corner and say their prayers right there! They were actually saying, "I'm so holy, I can't wait till I get to the synagogue to pray!" They received their reward – the praise of man (Matthew 6:5).

On the other hand, Jesus said to go into your closet, shut the door and pray to your Father who sees in secret. Then your Father will reward you openly (Matthew 6:6).

Prayer is rewarding. Even false prayers spoken for man's acclamation are rewarding. But from which source do you want your reward—man or God?

Habits

Oftentimes we fall into peculiar prayer habits. If we're impressed by a certain way a person prays, we'll incorporate their idiosyncrasies into our own prayers.

For instance, I may acquire a particular "prayer voice" by expressing my words with a little vibrato and sustain. "Oohh, God." Of course, I wouldn't dare talk to another person that way because he'd think I was weird. I wonder what I'd do if my kids would come to me and say, "Oohhh, dear Father!" Also, praying in Old English vocabulary sounds so much more spiritual. So, I revert to King James English instead of the Revised Standard for my prayers.

Jesus said that your Father knows what you need before you even ask Him (Matthew 6:8). So, just ask! God doesn't need to be sold a bill of goods. He's going to answer either yes or no, regardless of how you say it.

Jesus said, "*Ask* [please ask], *and ye shall receive*" (John 16:24). By asking, you open the door for God to do what He's wanted to do and to bless you like He's wanted to bless you all along.

Form for Prayer

Jesus gave us a basic form for prayer. "*After this manner therefore pray ye: Our Father...*" (Matthew 6:9). This prayer form immediately reveals that which is vital for effective prayer, a close personal relationship between the petitioner and God.

Your relationship to God is often manifested in how you address Him.

Some people begin their prayers with "Almighty God." If that's your relationship, then that's the way you should talk to Him. If you don't really know Him as your Father, then you should address Him as "Almighty God" or "Eternal God."

But, thank God, through Jesus Christ I can have a beautiful Father/son relationship. *"Behold, what manner of love the Father hath bestowed upon us, that we should be called the sons of God"* (1 John 3:1). Think of it! We've been called sons of God. I can now come to Him and say, "Father!"

But only through Jesus Christ can we be sons. Those outside of Jesus Christ have a distant relationship to the almighty, eternal God. But you, through Jesus Christ, have come into an intimate relationship. You may say, "Our Father, which art in heaven."

John said, *"As many as received him, to them gave he power to become the sons of God, even to them that believe on his name"* (John 1:12). God has given each of us *"the Spirit of adoption whereby we cry, Abba, Father. The Spirit itself beareth witness with our spirit that we are the children of God"* (Romans 8:15,16). Because I'm His child, I naturally call Him "Father." Relationship is of vital importance in prayer.

Jesus continues His model prayer with praise and worship. *"Hallowed be thy name"* (Matthew 6:9). Worship is an important part of prayer. *"Enter into his gates with thanksgiving, and into his courts with praise"* (Psalm 100:4). Too often we just rush right in and blurt out our requests. To enrich your prayer life, just praise Him for awhile. Then present your petitions.

The first two petitions in Jesus' model prayer are in the form of intercession. *"Thy kingdom come. Thy will be done"* (Matthew 6:10). Jesus said, *"Seek ye first the kingdom of God, and his righteousness; and all these [other] things [that you're so often praying about] shall be added unto you"* (Matthew 6:33). *"Delight thyself also in the LORD; and he shall give thee the desires of thine heart"* (Psalm 37:4).

So many times men seek happiness by direct pursuit. But happiness can never be discovered by direct pursuit. Happiness is the by-product of a personal relationship with God. If you have a right relationship with God, you will be filled with happiness.

In prayer, seek first the kingdom of God and His righteousness, and all these other things will be added to you. They'll be the by-product of a proper perspective of life. *"Thy kingdom come. Thy will be done."* Put those at the top of your list, and you'll find that God will take care of all the other things you've struggled with and have failed to accomplish.

You can come to God and make your needs and your requests known to Him. You can open your heart to Him and lay bear the innermost secrets of your soul. You can have such a blessed time by talking with the Father and finding His help, strength, and guidance.

What a privilege it is to pray! May God help you to discover the full, beautiful experience of prayer—not as a work, not as a task, not as a duty, not as a burden, not as an obligation—but the most joyous privilege in the world!

CHAPTER 4

EFFECTIVE PRAYER

The Bible teaches that faith produces answered prayer. Jesus said, *"What things soever ye desire, when ye pray, believe that ye receive them, and ye shall have them"* (Mark 11:24).

I find it easier to have faith for answered prayers when I realize the magnificent power of the One to whom I'm talking. In the Book of Acts the disciples prayed, *"Lord, thou art God, which hast made heaven, and earth, and the sea, and all that in them is"* (Acts 4:24).

When you pray you're actually talking to the divine Creator of this entire universe. Remember that! Too often we carry our own limitations over to God. Sometimes we know too much about the circumstances of a situation, and we have difficulty praying with faith.

For example, I have a mechanical mind. Therefore, it's very difficult for me to pray for a miracle when the engine in my car won't run. I just lack the faith that God can start the car when I know quite well that the coil is weak, the points are bad, and the battery has been run down. There's no way I can pray, "O God, help this car to start!"

However, my wife doesn't know a thing about mechanics. She's rarely looked under the hood of a car. She doesn't know a distributor from a carburetor or an oil dipstick from a radiator cap. So she can have great faith whenever we have trouble getting the car started.

I'll say, "What are we going to do?"

She'll say, "Let's pray."

I'll answer, "Aw, come on! We can't pray for something like this. It's mechanical."

But she'll bow her head and say, "Lord, help this car to start now. You know we've got to get going. I thank you, Father, and I ask it in Jesus' name." Then she'll say, "Okay. Try it again."

I'll say, "But it's no use!"

"Just go ahead and try it." And the engine will fire off!

Whom are you addressing when you pray? What limit can you place on God's ability? Look around the universe at what God has already done. Then figure out what His limitations might be. He's quite a big God.

We sometimes pray as if we were talking to someone extremely limited in power. "O, Lord! I don't know if You can do this or not. I even hate to ask You. And if You can't, well, that's all right. I understand."

Difficulty must always be measured by the capacity of the agent called upon to do the work. Who is the agent you're calling upon? He is God, the Creator of the universe. He is your heavenly Father who loves you and has a deep concern for you. Nothing is too hard for Him.

Jeremiah prayed, *"Lord God! behold, thou hast made the heaven and the earth by thy great power and stretched out arm, and there is nothing too hard for thee"* (Jeremiah 32:17). That's a good way to start prayer!

Many times we're too overburdened with the situation when we start to pray. It's been sitting on our shoulders and it feels like a thousand tons. We plead, "O Lord, what can move this mountain? You know what the doctor said about this, Lord. Fatal in 99% of the cases. O Lord, this is horrible!"

We're so taken back with the problem that we've forgotten that we're talking with the One who created the heavens, the earth, the sea, and everything that is in them. It's no more difficult for God to cure a person in the last stages of leukemia than it is for Him to take away a sore throat. It's no more difficult for God to put a new arm on a man than it is to remove his headache.

You may say, "Come on, now. There *are* limits."

What if a starfish lost one of his arms? Would you have a hard time praying, "God, put a new arm on that starfish?" No. We know that nature causes a new arm to grow on a starfish. Cut a little earthworm in half, and nature will make it grow another half. But who is nature? Who created the laws of nature? Could not God, who created us and all the functions within us, cause a new arm to grow? If He can put within the earthworm the capacity to grow another half, why would it be so difficult for Him to put a new arm or a new leg on a person?

When we think of such miracles, we're stymied from the human standpoint and carry that limit over to God. We say, "Don't bother about a new arm, God. Just help him adjust to living without it."

Sometimes God will perform miracles just to show us that He can do it in spite of our unbelief.

A lady called me one time in Tucson where I was pastoring. She said, "Oh, Chuck, pray for my little son, David. The car door slammed on his finger. We're at the doctor's office and he says he'll have to amputate! Please pray, Chuck, that God will heal it, and they won't have to amputate David's finger."

I prayed with the mother over the phone. The Spirit moved upon my heart and I really felt good about the situation. I said, "I believe God's going to heal David's finger! Praise the Lord and rejoice! God's going to do a miraculous work!"

The doctor told David's mother, "You can bring him back tomorrow. But we'll have to make the decision whether or not to amputate tomorrow."

The next day she took little David back to the specialist. He looked at the finger and said, "I'm sorry, but blood poisoning has already set in. I'm going to have to amputate. The bone is crushed and there's nothing else I can do."

She called me on the phone. She was crying so hard she couldn't talk. "What's the matter?" I asked. She was hysterical. Her sister took the phone and said, "Chuck, the doctor just amputated the tip of David's finger and it has her completely shaken."

I said, "Tell her I'll meet her at the house."

As I drove to her house I was so angry with God! I said, "Lord, why didn't You heal that finger? You could have healed it so easily! That's nothing for You. Besides, I told her to trust and have faith in You, and now look what You've done. You've let both of us down! I've got to go and talk to her now. She's hysterical and I don't know what to say!"

When I got to her house I said, "June, we know that all things work together for good to them that love God. God has a purpose.... It could have been his whole finger, or an arm. Be thankful it was just the tip of the finger. That isn't too bad. David will learn to adjust. Someday we'll discover God's purposes."

It's not easy to counsel in these situations, but I did the best I could. On my way home I was still angry with God. "Lord, I just don't understand what You're doing! If I were You, I certainly would have healed that finger."

I was upset. My faith was shattered. I couldn't have prayed for someone's cold that night. The faith of David's mother was shattered. Though I tried to comfort her, she couldn't be comforted.

The next morning she called me. She was very excited, screaming on the phone, "Chuck! Chuck! Something happened!"

I said, "What happened now?"

"It's fabulous!" she said. "David was wrestling with his brother and he knocked the bandage off his finger. I went to put the bandage back on. There's another whole pink fingertip growing out! It looks like brand new flesh!" She took David to the specialist. He looked at the finger and scratched his head. He said, "Nurse, bring me my chart." He looked at his chart and said, "Nurse, we did amputate, didn't we?"

She said, "Yes, doctor."

The doctor shook his head. "That's impossible!" he said. "Could you bring David back tomorrow, please?"

His mother brought David the next day and the doctor went through the same routine. He said, "Would you mind bringing him back tomorrow?" Every day for a week David's mother had to bring her little boy into the specialist who would look at the new fingertip and scratch his head. He X-rayed it and saw that the bone was intact. He said, "This is something fantastic! As far as I know, medical science has never seen anything like this. I have no explanation for it at all. But, of course, you know that it's impossible for a nail ever to form on that tip."

A couple of weeks later a fingernail started growing. Within two months David could hold out both hands, and you couldn't tell which finger tip had been amputated!

David went back to the doctor once a week for a year. The doctor took pictures, documented the whole event and submitted it to the Journal of the American Medical Association. The doctor was a Jew, and David's mother testified to him about the power of Jesus Christ. He finally said, "I have to confess that this is a miracle of God."

Afterwards I admitted, "Wow! You sure are smart, God! That's really far out!" Had God healed the finger before the amputation, the specialist would never have believed any part of the mother's witness. He would have rationalized that the body healed itself. But after the amputation... "You did it to blow the doctor's mind!"

Why do we limit God? Because we are limited. We need to realize to whom we're talking when we pray. Get our eyes off our problems. Get our minds on the fact that we're talking to the Creator of all things: God, who is so great, so vast, and so powerful!

God's Wisdom

As you pray, it is also important to realize the extent of God's wisdom. God knows everything about your life. He knows the troubles you're going through, the situations you're facing, and the problems you have.

In fact, thousands of years ago God knew the problems you'd be facing today. He also knew the answer He'd work out for you. God isn't taken by surprise. He isn't at a loss for an answer to your problems. God has your whole situation totally under His control.

Satan's actions do not diminish God's control, for Satan can do no more than what God allows him to do. God sets the boundaries for the enemy and says, "You can move in this box, but you can't go outside of it." All things are moving within the prescribed limits set by God.

Look at Russia, once one of the most powerful military forces in the world. Look at the armaments and megaton bombs she possessed, her delivery system of ICBM's and their tremendous power. The Russians were threatening not many years ago to bury us. But they can't even lift a bomb off the ground unless God allows them to do it. All things happen according to God's predetermined counsel. When you pray, remember that nothing is out of God's hand. God has everything under His control, and I might add, His timing is perfect though it is often not in sync with ours.

Once everything is in perspective and you realize to whom you're praying—how great God is, how wise He is, and how completely He controls all things—your requests won't seem so impossible.

"O Lord God, You created the heavens, the earth, the sea, and everything in them. You've got everything under control. You've written about today's world condition thousands of years ago. It's all happening right on target just as You predicted and according to Your counsel. O Lord, You know my tooth aches. Please take the pain away!" If God created the universe, it is certainly not hard for Him to take care of this little annoyance.

The greater our concept of God, the smaller our problem seems. However, most of the time we get right into the problem when we pray. "O, God! This is so big! This is so horrible!" We panic because the mountain seems so high. But God created Mt. Everest, and He could move it to another part of the universe if He so desired! Jesus said,

> *If ye have faith as a grain of mustard seed, ye shall say unto this mountain, Remove hence to yonder place; and it shall remove; and nothing shall be impossible unto you.*

> —Matthew 17:20

How big is that mountain you're facing? "I don't know how I'm going to pay my bills next week! Where will I ever get the money?" Where did all the gold come from anyway? God created it. It's nothing for God to meet your needs. If you can realize His power, His wisdom, His sovereignty, then you can bring your request to God with confidence and ease.

In the Old Testament, King Asa said, *"LORD, it is nothing with thee to help, whether with many, or with them that have no power"* (2

Chronicles 14:11). In other words, it really makes no difference to God whether you have a big army or a small platoon.

Early one morning Jonathan arose and saw Israel's enemies, the Philistines, camped in the distance. Most of Saul's army had deserted and fled across the Jordan river. He looked around and saw that the men in his own company were fast asleep. He nudged his armor-bearer and said, "Wake up! Look at all those Philistines over there. I wonder if God wants to deliver the Philistines to Israel today? If He does He doesn't need the whole army. He can deliver the Philistines to the two of us just as easily as to the whole army. Let's venture over to the Philistine camp and see if God wants to work for Israel today."

They came into the camp of the Philistines and began attacking them. These two fellows began the rout of the whole Philistine army! (1 Samuel 14:1–18) It makes no difference to God whether you're weak or strong, whether you have a whole army or you're alone. If God is doing the work, that's all that counts.

How do we engage in prayers that produce results? How can we pray effectively? Get the right concept of God—and the rest is easy!

CHAPTER 5

STRENGTH IN PRAYER

The strength of a believer is always related to his faith in God. Jesus said, *"Without me ye can do nothing"* (John 15:5). Unfortunately, I don't always believe that.

In fact, it seems that I often believe just the opposite. I stubbornly insist that there must be something good I can do apart from Jesus. I'm always looking for some redeeming quality within myself, some characteristic for which God might love me—because it seems that I'm incurably self-righteous. "That's all right, Lord, I'll do this one. You don't have to help me this time." Then when I totally fail, Jesus reminds me, *"Without me ye can do nothing."*

I have proven the truth of that statement over and over in my life. Apart from Christ I can do nothing. I am really weak and helpless.

On the other hand, I've discovered another beautiful truth, one that Paul also discovered. *"I can do all things through Christ which strengtheneth me"* (Philippians 4:13). Apart from Him I'm totally helpless and have no strength. Through Christ I have strength to meet any situation and to overcome any difficulty. In myself I am weak, but in Him I am strong.

Some people are strong within themselves. They trust in their own abilities and then gloat in their independence and strength. However, no matter how strong a person thinks he may be, there will come a day when he exhausts his own resources and finally confesses, "I can't do it! I can't go on!"

When the man who has learned to trust only in himself comes to that day of reckoning, it is a tragic and disastrous day. But for the man who has learned to trust in the Lord, that day is no different than any other, because he has learned to turn every day over to God. The man who is self-reliant, self-willed, and self-made will ultimately fall. But the man who has learned to trust in the Lord for his strength will never fall. As long as I am looking to myself and my own resources, I will always be restricted by my human limitations. But if I trust in God and in His resources, then I have His infinite capacities available to me.

I can never face a situation which is too big for God and me to handle. There is no obstacle so great that God and I can't overcome. There is no enemy too strong for God and I to defeat. God and I make a majority in any crowd! If God be for me, who can be against me? (Romans 8:31). Learn to turn to God for your resources and your strength. In 2 Corinthians 12:9, Paul is speaking of his infirmities or weaknesses. He speaks of glorying in his weaknesses that the power of Christ might rest upon him. He said that he actually took pleasure in his weaknesses, for when he was weak then he was strong. My greatest area of weakness is where I feel strongest in my flesh and in no need of the Lord's help. Conversely, my greatest area of strength is where I know that I am weak and cannot make it without the Lord's help.

God is our source of strength. Prayer is the channel through which God gives His strength.

Prayer in Action

Nehemiah was a man of the Word and prayer. When Hanani and the other travelers returned from Jerusalem, Nehemiah questioned them about his beloved city. Hanani told him of the bad state of affairs in Jerusalem. "The walls are broken down. The people are demoralized. They're barely existing. They're an easy prey to all of their enemies. They have no defenses. The city is in shambles!"

When Nehemiah heard the condition of Jerusalem, God's holy city, he wept before the Lord. Then Nehemiah fasted, prayed, and confessed to God his sins and the sins of the people. He also acknowledged the righteousness of God's judgment against Jerusalem. Notice how he used the Word of God in his prayer. He said, "Lord, You said by the mouth of Moses that if we turn from You, You would turn Your back upon us and make us afraid of our enemies, and we would be scattered into the world. But, Lord, You also said that if we would turn back to You and seek Your face and call upon You, You would hear us and restore and rebuild the land" (Nehemiah 1:1–11).

The burden on Nehemiah's heart was to restore and rebuild the city of Jerusalem. The Bible shows us how God opened the doors for Nehemiah's prayer to be answered.

Nehemiah was the cupbearer to the king of Persia in Shushan. This prestigious position brought him into daily contact with the king. One day as he bore the cup to the king, the king asked, "Nehemiah, why are you looking so sad today? I've never seen you so glum."

Nehemiah replied, "I've just received the report concerning Jerusalem. It is devastated and the people are demoralized. How can I be happy when the city I love is so desolate?"

The king said, "What would you like me to do?"

Nehemiah tells us, *"I prayed to the God of heaven. And I said unto the king…"* When the king said, "What can I do for you?" Nehemiah prayed, "Quick, God, help! What do I say?" (Nehemiah 2:1–4).

Nehemiah prayed first and then acted. That is the correct order: pray, then act. If we always prayed before we acted, needless to say, we would act differently in many cases. We wouldn't be so apt to act rashly or inappropriately. The Bible promises, *"In all thy ways acknowledge him, and he shall direct thy paths"* (Proverbs 3:6). Prayer was such an important part of Nehemiah's life that it was simultaneous with his actions.

Nehemiah's response to the king's question was to ask for permission to rebuild the walls of Jerusalem. The king granted Nehemiah's request, and sent him to Jerusalem with a company of men.

As Nehemiah and his men were rebuilding the wall, their enemies gathered around them and tried to defeat the Israelites by ridiculing them and mocking the construction of the wall. Many times Satan uses ridicule to discourage you in the work of God. He says, "Who do you think you are? Billy Graham? Are you out to save the world?" Ridicule is one of the main tools the enemy uses to thwart your efforts for God. And it's a powerful tool. None of us like to be ridiculed. Too often that device actually stops a person's ministry for God.

But Nehemiah did the right thing. Instead of battling the enemy himself and answering the mockery, he prayed, "Lord, You've heard them. Take care of them. Wipe them out. Lead them into captivity" (Nehemiah 4:1–5). Don't respond to ridicule by striking back. It's much better to commit it to the Lord and let Him be your defense. You'll surely be strong in Him.

When the enemy realized that they couldn't discourage the rebuilding of the wall through ridicule, they planned to attack and tear it down at night. Nehemiah heard of the conspiracy and replied. *"We made our prayer unto our God, and set a watch against them day and night"* (Nehemiah 4:9).

This brings out an important point. Prayer should never be an excuse for idleness or foolhardy action. God has given you good common sense and He expects you to use it. If you're being threatened by an enemy, pray first—but then take what defensive measures are necessary. Action following prayer is not a lack of faith.

Be practical. If you ask God to heal your poor eyesight, don't throw away your eyeglasses before the optometrist has a chance to retest you and says that you've been healed. Prayer shouldn't lead you into reckless or careless actions. It should actually create a diligence within you. In fact, prayer will lead you into activity more often than it will lead you into inactivity. Pray first, then take action.

Some people are very lazy and think that God is going to do all the work for them. You question them about something and they use the excuse, "I'm just leaving that in the hands of the Lord." No, the Lord expects you to act, too!

For instance, if you need a job, you don't just sit at home and wait for someone to call. You ask God to give you one. Then go out and submit applications every place you can. Then trust that the Lord will open the door to the job He wants you to have. Don't just sit there and say, "Okay, Lord, bring me the job." You don't say that when you have to eat. You don't lie in bed and say, "If you want me to eat today, Lord, just drop the food in my mouth." You're not passive about that, and you shouldn't be passive about the other areas of your life.

"So we prayed unto God," Nehemiah said, *"and we set a watch against the enemy."* The Israelites built the wall with a trowel in one hand and a sword in the other. The enemy saw that they were armed and prepared, so he didn't attack; instead, he planned new ways for Jerusalem's destruction.

Nehemiah, knowing the enemy was trying to weaken him and the hands of his men, prayed, *"God, strengthen my hands"* (Nehemiah 6:9). Nehemiah, a man of prayer, was a man of action and of strength as a result.

Man of Prayer

What constitutes a man of prayer? First, he prays about everything—little things as well as big things. Oftentimes, we're reluctant to pray about the little things because we're afraid to bother God with trivia. He's so busy running the universe that He doesn't need to help me in the small areas of my life. But Jesus said that our heavenly Father is conscious of the sparrow falling to the ground. How much more is He conscious of our every need? (Luke 12:6–7).

The Bible also commands, *"In every thing by prayer and supplication with thanksgiving let your requests be made known unto God"* (Philippians 4:6). If you really love someone, it doesn't matter how often he calls or what he calls about, you're just glad to hear from him. God loves you so much, He doesn't care how trivial your need might be. He just loves to hear from you.

Jesus said, *"Men ought always to pray, and not to faint"* (Luke 18:1). Why then are so many people losing heart and never praying? I hear people say, "I don't know what I'm going to do! I don't know where to turn." They're fainting. Learn of God's grace through prayer. Learn to turn every situation over to God so your life might be strengthened by His hand upon you.

As a result of Nehemiah's close fellowship with God, the walls of Jerusalem were rebuilt in fifty-two days. Others had tried to rebuild those same walls for almost a hundred years! Not only that, there was a spiritual revival among the people. While doing the physical work of God, Nehemiah and his men also did a spiritual work. The Israelites became so excited that their walls were rebuilt and they could again dwell securely in Jerusalem that they gathered together to worship the Lord. In the temple, Ezra the scribe brought out the law of God and read it to the people. It was accompanied by repentance and weeping before God. The hearts of the people were turned back to the Lord (Nehemiah 8–9).

One man living in prayer and fellowship with God can accomplish incredible results!

As I look around today, I see that we're living in a needy world. We need people who live in fellowship with God, who know the strength of God, and who are willing to pray for God's work to be done. Why not be that man of prayer for the sake of this poor, lost world, nation, city, school, or perhaps even your own family.

CHAPTER 6

PRAY, AND I WILL ANSWER

I am always interested in the prayers we find in the Bible. And I'm especially interested in those prayers that produced results. The prayer of Jabez in the Old Testament is one such example. In studying his words, we can learn some valuable insights into prayer.

Which God Do You Serve?

First of all, the Bible declares that when Jabez prayed, he *"called on the God of Israel"* (1 Chronicles 4:10). What God do you call upon when you pray?

I've met people who live very carelessly and recklessly. From outward observances they lead very sinful lives. When we start talking and they realize that I'm a minister, they usually interject, "I know that I'm not living like I should, but I pray every night. I never go to sleep without saying my prayers."

When these people pray, "Now I lay me down to sleep, I pray thee Lord…" —whom are they addressing? Who is the true "Lord" of their lives?

"Lord" is not so much a name as it is a title. People serve many different gods, many different lords. Who is the lord of your life? It's important to know the one you're addressing in your prayers. Jesus said that not all who say, "Lord, Lord" are even going to enter the kingdom of heaven.

God told Jeremiah that when the people of Israel call to Him, He would no longer hear them. The next time they're in trouble, they were not to ask God for help. Let them call on the gods that they've been serving (Jeremiah 11:12,14). Thus when Israel cried, "O god, help us," they might have been calling on Baal, or Molech, or Ashtoreth.

It's a tragic day when God finally says to a man, "I've had it! You've lived a careless life and you've worshipped and served everything but Me, but when you're in trouble you call on Me. Next time you're in trouble, just call on the gods you've been serving."

Your god is really the supreme passion of your life. For instance, many people today worship and serve their intellects. "To know and to understand," they say, "is the greatest good. I cannot accept the idea of a supreme being because I do not believe in anything I cannot bring into the confines of my mind." Therefore, when they pray, "O god," they're actually praying to their own intellects.

In ancient times people named and worshipped a multitude of gods. But we're too sophisticated today to give ancient names to our gods. A person today might serve his passions but, if asked who his god is, he wouldn't say,

"Venus, the goddess of love." He'd just say, "I'm a lover. I believe a person should seek the best things of life. Love is the ultimate. Therefore, to make love is the chief goal of man." When he cries, "O god," he might as well be crying "O Venus!"

There are others who deify the pleasure principle. They live and work the entire week with one thing on their mind: the weekend. "Friday night we'll get in the camper—with the three wheeler on the back, the boat on top, and the dune buggy behind—and we'll head out for the river! Wow, what a weekend we'll have!" All week long they're thinking of the thrills, excitement, and pleasures they'll have on the weekend. Every night they tinker around at home in preparation to go Friday night.

There was an ancient faith whose believers also worshipped pleasure. They called their god Molech. Many people today, when they cry "O god," are actually crying to Molech because, in reality, he is their god.

There are others who deify the power principle. "Might is right." They seek to possess and to have. They're constantly scheming to get more money in order to get more possessions.

Their minds are always analyzing how to cut this, increase that, invest here or there. They take second jobs. Their interests are centered around money, money, and more money. This is the worship of the old god Mammon. When these people are in trouble, they cry, "O god!" But their god Mammon can't hear.

It's important to realize that the prospect of your prayers being answered is totally dependent upon the one whom you petition. You might tell me, "Chuck, I need one hundred thousand dollars. You don't know how desperately I need it. If I don't get it, I don't know what I'm going to do!"

You could plead with me for a whole week, two weeks, or two years, but you don't have a chance of getting that amount from me. I just don't have it. You're petitioning someone who has no power or capacity to answer.

When the prophets of Baal were beseeching their god to send fire to their altar, they cried all morning. "O Baal, send fire!" But there was no fire. About noon Elijah said, "Fellows, I bet the problem is that your god has gone someplace. Or else he's sleeping. Why don't you cry a little louder? Maybe then he'll hear you." They started crying louder, and soon they were cutting themselves and leaping on their altar to get Baal's attention! (1 Kings 18:26–29). They could have gone on forever, and still no fire would have come down to consume their sacrifice. Why? Because their god had no capacity to answer.

Deification of love, money, pleasure, or intellect is to deify impersonal, impotent forces. In the hour of real need these gods can produce nothing. But when I cry to Jehovah, the God of Israel, I know that he is able to do far more abundantly than all that I ask or think (Ephesians 3:20). There's no end to God's power. When I cry to Him, He is able to meet my needs. "One hundred thousand dollars?" He asks. "Is that all?" It's nothing for God to meet my need, no matter what it might be.

When Jehovah God is the agent I call upon, nothing is too difficult for Him. But if Venus, Molech, Mammon, or Baal are the agents I call upon to do a work, then I'm really in a bind. In the hour of real need, when I cry in desperation, they just aren't there to help.

Life is so empty for the people who live for pleasure. I've stood beside many people in their time of need. When their child is lying on a hospital bed and the doctor walks out of the operating room shaking his head, they look at me as if to say, "Do something, preacher!" Their god of pleasure is so empty at that time. He has so little comfort, help, or hope to offer.

But when you worship Jehovah and call upon Him as your Lord, it's glorious to know that He is able to help. And not only able to help, but willing and wanting to help.

Paul said to the Athenians on Mars Hill, that the God he wanted to talk to them about, the One they called the unknown God, is the One who created the heavens and the earth and everything in them. *"In Him we live, and move, and have our being"* (Acts 17:22–28). That's the One I cry to when I call upon God—the One who rules me and is Lord of my life.

Petitions of Jabez

Now let's look at Jabez's petitions. First of all, Jabez called upon the God of Israel, saying, *"O, that thou wouldest bless me"* (1 Chronicles 4:10). Jabez wasn't ashamed to say, "Bless me." And I'm not ashamed to ask God to bless me. I want God to bless me. I want every blessing that

God has for me. If I'm to be a blessing to others I must first receive the blessings of God.

Now notice the blessings that Jabez requested. First of all he said, *"Enlarge my coast"* (1 Chronicles 4:10). The Jews had come into the Promised Land, but much of the land was in the hands of the enemy. God had promised them the entire land, but they had not yet obtained the full promise of God. Thus Jabez prayed, "Lord, enlarge my coast," or actually, "Help me to possess all that You've given me."

I pray this in my own life. "Lord, help me to possess all that You have given and promised to me." God has given to us rich and precious promises. We can be living in a glorious spiritual atmosphere, as we live in the heavenlies in Christ Jesus. But instead we choose to drag along on the bottom of the pile, groveling in the dirt. You may enjoy it down here, but I enjoy it up there. Thus I pray, "Lord, bless me and help me to possess all that You have given to me. I thank You for what You've already done for me, Lord, but You've promised so much more..."

After all, why should you close the door on what God wants to do for you? Some people say, "I really don't feel I need the gifts of the Spirit." Personally, I need everything that God has to give me. Not only do I need everything that God has offered to give me, I desire everything that He has to give.

When I come to God, I don't close any doors. I say, "Okay, Lord, here I am. Do things Your way. Don't let me put any restrictions in Your path. Enlarge my coast, and allow me to possess all that You have promised." Whenever I try to dictate to God what blessings I will accept, and which I reject, I'm actually exalting my own wisdom above His. I'm saying that I know my needs better than He knows. "You can do this and this for me, God, but I don't want You to do that."

Not me! I pray, "Enlarge my coast, Lord. Bless me. Do all that You want to do in my life."

Then Jabez prayed, *"That thine hand might be with me"* (1 Chronicles 4:10). It is so important that I have the hand of God upon my life in all the things I do. It's dangerous to undertake any project without God's hand upon me.

Moses said to the Lord, *"If thy presence go not with me, carry us not up hence"* (Exodus 33:15).

Lord, don't lead me anywhere You're not going to be with me. I can go forth with assurance, comfort, and power when I know that God's hand is upon my life. I need no longer tremble.

Jabez's next petition was, *"Keep me from evil"* (1 Chronicles 4:10). This is such an important prayer that Jesus included it as the last petition in the Lord's Prayer. *"Deliver us from evil"* (Matthew 6:13). The evil one is always trying to draw us into his snare.

I so easily fall into the snare of the enemy and allow hatred to begin to master my life, bitterness to control me, or some evil way to get its grip upon me. It's difficult to live a righteous life. In fact, it's not possible by our own human energy. It takes the power of the Spirit of God in me to live righteously.

Then Jabez continued, *"Keep me from evil, that it may not grieve me"* (1 Chronicles 4:10). The primary result of evil is very rarely grief. The primary result of evil is quite often thrills and excitement. Evil often has the appearance of being very prosperous. "It looks like such an easy way to make a quick buck. Of course, it isn't quite honest. But look at the profits you can make. And look at what you can do with the money that you get from the profits!"

The primary result of evil may be joy, excitement, pleasure, or possessions—but the end result of evil is always grief. You may not think so right now. Sin may seem very exciting to you today. But a wise man will always consider the final destination of the path he is taking. Where is your path leading you? If it is a path of evil, my friend, it is leading you to grief. In Psalm 73, Asaph said that he was envious of the foolish when he saw the prosperity of the wicked. This almost stumbled him in his walk and commitment to the Lord until he considered the end results of their wickedness.

In the Proverbs, Solomon warned his son about the prostitute.

> *The lips of a strange woman drop as an honeycomb, and her mouth is smoother than oil: But her end is bitter...her feet go down to death; her steps take hold on hell.*

> —Proverbs 5:3–5

At first glance sin may look exciting, but the end result is death and hell. Solomon declared, *"There is a way which seemeth right unto a man, but* the end thereof are the ways of death" (Proverbs 14:12).

Answers

What was the result of Jabez's prayer? The Bible said, *"God granted him that which he requested."* Praise the Lord! Jabez asked God to bless him and God did bless him. He asked the Lord to enlarge his coast and the Lord enlarged his coast. Jabez said, "Lord, keep your hand upon me," and God kept His hand on him. He said, "Lord keep me from evil," and the Lord kept him from evil.

It's glorious to know that I can pray and if I pray according to the will of God, the Bible promises,

> *If we ask any thing according to his will, he heareth us: and if we know that he hear us, whatsoever we ask, we know that we have the petitions that we desired of him.*
>
> —1 John 5:14–15

I can pray with confidence for God to bless me, enlarge my coast, keep His hand upon me, and keep me from evil—for this is the will of God for my life.

Ask Him and you, too, shall receive. Jesus said, "*Ask* [please ask], *and ye shall receive, that your joy may be full*" (John 16:24).

CHAPTER 7

SIN OF PRAYERLESSNESS

In your walk with the Lord, God will lift you up to the highest level you allow Him, and He'll do His best for you on that level. But, unfortunately, so many times we limit what God wants to do in our lives by insisting on our own way instead of yielding to His way. God would do so much more for us, but so many times we're too busy insisting, "This is the way I want it, God!" In demanding my own way, I go from

God's best to second or third best. His work in my life is often limited because I reject His divine way.

Such was the case with Israel. Israel was once a theocracy, a nation governed by God. But the time came in Israel's history when the people no longer wanted God to rule over them. They demanded a king like all the other nations. This was a time of national disaster as Israel deteriorated from a theocracy to a monarchy.

God accommodated the demands of the people and commanded Samuel to anoint Saul as king. God did not wipe out the Israelites and say, "I'm through with you!" They were still God's people. He did the best He could under their imposed conditions...and He appointed a king for Israel.

However, God wanted them to know that He was displeased with their decision. Through Samuel He told them that He was going to send rain on their wheat fields. The rain came and the people grew fearful. They cried to Samuel, their prophet, "We've sinned! Pray to God for us that we will not die, for we have added to all of our other sins by asking for a king."

Samuel answered, "Don't be afraid. Even though you have sinned, you're still God's people. He has chosen you for His name's sake." Then he said these amazing words:

> *Moreover as for me, God forbid that I should sin against the* LORD *in ceasing to pray for you.*
>   —1 Samuel 12:16–23

According to this passage, it is actually a sin not to pray. How many times are we guilty of the sin of prayerlessness! Think of what a reproach it is to God when you do not pray.

God is the Creator of the universe. *"All things were made by him; and without him was not any thing made that was made"* (John 1:3). The One who has created this vast universe has given you an invitation to come, talk, and fellowship with Him. He has invited you to enter into His presence to share any problems or needs you might have. Yet, so many times we ignore this invitation.

Imagine that in your mail was a letter which had the engraved, full-color, embossed seal of the President of the United States. You tear open the letter and find a formal invitation to the White House with all expenses paid. What would you do? Toss it away? No. The President, whether you agree with him or not, is an important person. Would you fail to respond? Of course not.

If you respond to a human being's invitation with graciousness, think of the reproach when God, who has invited you to come and have fellowship with Him, is refused.

You may say, "I just don't have time to pray." Do you have time to watch television? We have time to do the things we really want to do. Therefore, God must assume that we really don't want to fellowship with Him. And that's a correct assumption.

Our flesh rebels against prayer because it's an exercise of the spirit. That is why I get so tired as soon as I start to pray. I say, "I'm too sleepy, Lord." My flesh is rebelling against the spiritual exercise of prayer.

The spirit and flesh are always warring against each other. Whenever I enter into spiritual exercise, my flesh rebels against it. I find any excuse possible. "I'm too upset to pray" or "I'm too weak to pray."

Prayerlessness actually hinders the work of God. You may ask, "Isn't God sovereign? Can't

He do whatever He wants to do? Doesn't He rule over the entire universe? Aren't His purposes going to be accomplished no matter what? Then how can prayerlessness hinder the work of God?"

It is true that God is sovereign. But it's also true that God has created us as free moral agents. We have the capacity to choose and act freely, and God respects your free moral agency. He will not force His will nor His desires upon your life. He has given you the ability to choose, and He honors your choice.

God has ordained that His work on earth be wrought through prayer and by our agreeing together in prayer.

In Psalms it declares that the Hebrew nation *"limited the Holy One of Israel"* (Psalm 78:41). An unlimited God was limited by man's unbelief. What is it that keeps you from prayer? Unbelief. You can actually limit the work God wants to do by your unbelief.

Jesus said,

> *Ye have not chosen me, but I have chosen you, and ordained you, that ye should go and bring forth fruit, and that your fruit should remain:*

*that whatsoever ye shall ask of the Father in my
name, he may give it you.*

—John 15:16

God wants to give you many things, but He
will not give them until you pray. By prayer
you're actually opening the door to let God do
the things He wants to do. I believe we have
seen only a small fraction of what God has
wanted to do—because of our lack of prayer.

God commands us to pray. Therefore, not to
pray is an act of disobedience against God. The
Bible says, *"Pray without ceasing"* (1
Thessalonians 5:17), and *"Men ought always to
pray, and not to faint"* (Luke 18:1). Failure to pray
is a sin because I am disobeying the actual
command of God.

We need to pray for one another. It is a sin if
I, as a pastor, fail to pray for my flock. The
Scripture says, *"Pray one for another"* (James
5:16). *"Bear ye one another's burdens, and so fulfill
the law of Christ"* (Galatians 6:2).

Sometimes, we may pray about a certain
problem in another person's life. When the
problem doesn't immediately go away, we
become so discouraged that we decide to quit
praying for him altogether. We become so upset

with other people's failures, even though we may have the same faults in our lives. Our sins always look horrible when someone else is committing them!

Samuel had prayed that God would change the people's minds so they would no longer insist on a king. Samuel wanted God to rule and reign over the nation. But after all his prayers the children of Israel still insisted on a king. Samuel easily could have become disgusted and said, "I'm not going to pray for those stubborn, stiff-necked people anymore! They have what they asked for. Let them reap the consequences." But he didn't. He said to them, *"God forbid that I should sin against the Lord in ceasing to pray for you"* (1 Samuel 12:23).

Causes of Prayerlessness

If you examine yourself, you'll find a variety of reasons for the lack of prayer in your life. The first cause is the lack of time.

In this society we've allowed ourselves to become busier than God originally intended. When the Lord first created our bodies He intended for man to live at a much easier, more relaxed pace than we live today. Today, our lifestyle and our society make it difficult to find time to be alone with the Lord.

Also, it is extremely difficult to find an undisturbed place to pray. It's getting harder and harder to find a quiet place to be alone with the Lord. This world is becoming more congested and overcrowded, and Satan does everything he can to interrupt any quiet times you may have with the Lord.

For instance, you may go for a week without one telephone call. But, if you get lonesome and want the telephone to ring, just kneel down and pray. It may be a wrong number, but you can be sure the telephone is going to ring, or someone will be at the front door, or one of the children will come in crying. So many disturbances make it difficult to pray.

Another hindrance to prayer is the tendency to let your mind wander. You begin to pray about certain things. Quite soon your mind has taken you surfing—the waves are great, that next set looks like a beauty—oops, "Sorry, Lord!" Your mind has taken a little side journey.

Another problem which causes a lack of prayer is drowsiness. We live under such pressure most of the time that any free moment is a moment to rest. For instance, if you kneel down beside your bed and put your head in your arms and start to pray—that's a real good position to sleep! You soon doze off in the middle of a prayer. After a while your legs and knees begin to ache. It wakes you up. You suddenly realize, "I've been sleeping on the job!"

It's even worse if you decide to lie in bed and pray with your head on the pillow. Now, I don't discourage that completely. I go to sleep every night talking to the Lord. I enjoy communing with the Lord till I'm asleep. But it is necessary to have a prayer time that's much more active and alert.

Solutions

What can we do to overcome our problem of prayerlessness? I have a few practical suggestions. As far as time is concerned, we must discipline ourselves and take time for prayer. You'll never find time to pray. You must make time.

Life is made up of priorities. Since you can never do all that you want to do, you must always sacrifice the less important things for the more important ones. A wise man makes good use of his time and keeps his priorities in proper perspective.

Prayer is the most important activity you could ever engage in. It should be at the top of your priority list of things to do. You need to take the time for prayer even if you have to skip your time to eat or read the evening newspaper!

Secondly, find a place that is undisturbed. It may take some doing, but make the effort. Many times I go for a walk or take a drive to get alone with the Lord. I also wake up much earlier than the rest of my family. Prayer is more important to me than my sleep, and the phone rings very seldom in the early morning.

To keep my mind from wandering, I usually vocalize my prayers. It's true that God knows what's in my heart, but when I try to pray out of my heart my mind often wanders. For a moment I'm thinking, "Lord, take care of this and that. Thank you for this..." and pretty soon I'm surfing again! But when I vocalize my prayer, I have to think about what I'm saying. That causes me to concentrate on my conversation with the Lord.

I've found that it's best for me to pray while sitting in a chair. I don't even close my eyes because that can get dangerous!

As a child I was always told that if I didn't close my eyes, the Lord wouldn't hear me. A pastor once mentioned that when he was playing basketball in junior high, the team decided to pray before the game. Some kid said, "All right, everybody close your eyes or we'll lose." He peeked to see if they were all closing their eyes—and they lost. He felt guilty over that game for years!

However, in the Scriptures we are told to pray without ceasing (1 Thessalonians 5:17), which certainly indicates that prayer is not a position of the body. If I have to kneel down to pray, prayer without ceasing would mean that I would never get off my knees. Likewise, God does not expect us always to pray with our eyes closed, because prayer without ceasing would mean that I would never again open my eyes! Whether my eyes are open or closed, God hears all my prayers just the same.

I have found a good solution to drowsiness or sleepiness while praying is walking. As I'm walking I can't fall asleep. Sometimes I even walk back and forth in a room. Other times I go for a walk in a field or in the yard and talk to God. Some of my most fruitful and blessed prayer times have been during walks.

When I pray I talk to God just like I talk to my closest friend. I don't use any fancy tones or get wild and yell. God knows the real me. I don't need a "prayer tone." I talk to Him in a very matter-of-fact way. I tell Him all my problems, doubts, and questions. I try to be as honest with Him as I can. I might as well because He knows if I'm not! If I try to gloss over something, the only one who's getting fooled is me. God isn't fooled.

I may say, "Lord, you know I don't really have the depth of love for this fellow that I should have." This is an attempt to hide the truth and make me look not as bad as I am. I might as well tell Him the truth. "God, I hate him. I can't stand him. I'd like to punch him in the nose every time I see him!" Be honest, and then repent!

Also, I talk to God in a conversational way. This means that I must listen, too. After all, God wants to talk back to me. I find such joy and blessings as I come into this communion and fellowship with the One who created me.

May God forgive us our sin of prayerlessness. May God help us to pray fervently. And may we see the mighty work of God accomplished in this desperate world through our prayerfulness.

How to Become a Christian

First of all you must recognize that you are a sinner. Realize that you have missed the mark. This is true of each of us. We have deliberately crossed the line not once, but many times. The Bible says, *"All have sinned and fallen short of the glory of God"* (Romans 3:23). This is a hard admission for many to make, but if we are not willing to hear the bad news, we cannot appreciate and respond to the *good news*.

Second, we must realize that Jesus Christ died on the cross for us. Because of sin, God had to take drastic measures to reach us. So He came to this earth and walked here as a man. But Jesus was more than just a good man. He was the God-man—God incarnate—and that is why His death on the cross is so significant.

At the cross, God Himself—in the person of Jesus Christ—took our place and bore our sins. He paid for them and purchased our redemption.

Third, we must repent of our sin. God has commanded men everywhere to repent. Acts 3:19 states, *"Repent therefore and be converted, that your sins may be blotted out, so that times of refreshing may come from the presence of the Lord."* What does this word *repent* mean? It means to change direction–to hang a U-turn on the road of life. It means to stop living the kind of life we led previously and start living the kind of life outlined in the pages of the Bible. Now we must change and be willing to make a break with the past.

Fourth, we must receive Jesus Christ into our hearts and lives. Being a Christian is having God Himself take residence in our lives. John 1:12 tells us, *"But as many as received Him, to them He gave the right to become children of God."* We must receive Him. Jesus said, *"Behold, I stand at the door and knock. If anyone hears My voice and opens the door, I will come in..."* (Revelation 3:20). Each one of us must individually decide to open the door. How do we open it? Through prayer.

If you have never asked Jesus Christ to come into your life, you can do it right now. Here is a suggested prayer you might even pray.

Lord Jesus, I know that I am a sinner and I am sorry for my sin. I turn and repent of my sins right now. Thank You for dying on the cross for me and paying the price for my sin. Please come into my heart and life right now. Fill me with Your Holy Spirit and help me to be Your disciple. Thank You for forgiving me and coming into my life. Thank You that I am now a child of Yours and that I am going to heaven. In Jesus' name, I pray. Amen.

When you pray that prayer God will respond. You have made the right decision–the decision that will impact how you spend eternity. Now you will go to heaven, and in the meantime, find peace and the answers to your spiritual questions.

Taken from: *Life. Any Questions?*
by Greg Laurie, Copyright © 1995. Used by permission.

Other books available in this series...

Spiritual Warfare
by Brian Brodersen
Pastor Brian Brodersen of Calvary Chapel Costa Mesa, California brings biblical balance and practical insight to the subject of spiritual warfare. 73 pages

The Psychologizing of the Faith
by Bob Hoekstra
Pastor Bob Hoekstra of Living in Christ Ministries calls the church to leave the broken cisterns of human wisdom, and to return to the fountain of living water flowing from our wonderful counselor, Jesus Christ. 74 pages

Practical Christian Living
by Wayne Taylor
Pastor Wayne Taylor of Calvary Fellowship in Seattle, Washington takes us through a study of Romans 12 and 13 showing us what practical Christian living is all about. 152 pages

Building Godly Character
by Ray Bentley
Pastor Ray Bentley of Maranatha Chapel in San Diego, California takes us through a study in the life of David to show how God builds His character in our individual lives. 88 pages

Worship and Music Ministry
by Rick Ryan & Dave Newton
Pastor Rick Ryan and Dave Newton of Calvary Chapel Santa Barbara, California give us solid biblical insight into the important subjects of worship and music ministry within the body of Christ. 90 pages

Overcoming Sin & Enjoying God
by Danny Bond
Pastor Danny Bond of Pacific Hills Church in Aliso Viejo, California shows us, through practical principles, that it is possible to live in victory over sin and have constant fellowship with our loving God. 90 pages

Answers for the Skeptic
by Scott Richards
Pastor Scott Richards of Calvary Fellowship in Tucson, Arizona shows us what to say when our faith is challenged, and how to answer the skeptic in a way that opens hearts to the love and truth of Jesus Christ. 55 pages

The Afterglow
by Henry Gainey
Pastor Henry Gainey of Calvary Chapel Thomasville, Georgia gives instruction in conducting and understanding the proper use of the gifts of the Holy Spirit in an "Afterglow Service." 152 pages

Final Curtain
by Chuck Smith
Pastor Chuck Smith of Calvary Chapel Costa Mesa, California provides insight into God's prophetic plan and shows how current events are leading to the time when one climactic battle will usher in eternity. 96 pages

Creation by Design
by Mark Eastman, M.D.
Mark Eastman, M.D., of Genesis Outreach in Temecula, California, carefully examines and clarifies the evidence for a Creator God, as he shows the reader the amazing hand of design in creation. 62 pages

For ordering information, please contact:
The Word For Today
P.O. Box 8000, Costa Mesa, CA 92628
(800) 272-WORD
Also, visit us on the Internet at:
www.twft.com